The Little Guide
To Dreaming
BIG

Becky Schade

Table of Contents

Introduction

Groan when the alarm goes off. Get ready for work in a daze. Count down the hours on the job until it's time to go home. Rush out the door to buy a little time for chores on the way. Squeeze in time with the family in the evening. Stay up a little too late trying to unwind before bed. Spend the weekend trying to forget about the weekdays. Rinse. Repeat.

It's a scene that plays out every day across the world, what many would consider an ordinary existence. But for some individuals, this busy routine becomes unbearable. These people coast through their lives as if they were playing a role, never fully invested and wondering what else is out there. They feel trapped by the conventions of society, and search for something better.

I'd like to pose a question to you. Why do we live? What is the purpose of life?

To pass on our genes? Sure. All life forms have a biological imperative to reproduce. But with the self-awareness that humanity has achieved I think we can all agree that cannot be all there is to life.

To survive, then? That might sound ridiculous in our first-world country, but think about it. We're taught that a person needs to do well in school so that they can get a good job. We need to work hard to stay ahead of the game because the competition is fierce. We should then buy a big house and other symbols that showcase our status to let the rest of the world know that we're winning. And we need to hide the parts of ourselves that don't fit the status quo because *different* is bad.

We join in the rat race because we've been told that way lies security. We've been conditioned to believe that a

4

person can never have enough, whether of money, power, or fame. The more you have, the better off you'll be in the future.

And so our default purpose in life becomes an endless search for safety.

Security is comfortable, but it doesn't bring joy or make us feel alive. And that's what we're looking for, deep down. Not to float along on the sea of "just surviving," but to truly feel alive.

We've been told that the responsibilities of adulthood have to come before our own desires, but that doesn't make it the truth. The people who love their life are those who have found a way to integrate both responsibilities and desires into a more meaningful existence that fulfills them and helps others at the same time.

It's time to give your dreams the attention they deserve. It's time to live.

Part 1
Six Steps to Success

Deciding to take your dreams seriously is a lot easier said than done. Some people don't even know what exactly their dreams are at the beginning, they just know something needs to change. But no matter where you are in the process, this guide is designed to see you though with as little pain as possible.

There are two basic phases to achieving your dreams: the *discovery phase*, and the *action phase*. In Part 1 we'll address the discovery phase, which covers the research and planning necessary for success.

This section is divided into six steps. We'll uncover your guiding values as a way to really zero in on what your big dreams are. We'll get specific about the cost of your dreams in money and time, and how to free up more of both. And we'll create a plan of attack that eliminates confusion and lets you know exactly what needs to be done next to accomplish them.

Step 1: Discover your guiding values

When you think of values, you might think about being honest, or kind, or hard-working—ideals that we've all been taught to strive for. But this isn't about self-improvement: this is a question of who you *are*.

Despite the fact that we should be more familiar with ourselves than anyone else, this is still an uncomfortable topic for most people. It takes a lot of guts to look inward at what makes us tick, because we compare ourselves to the ideal of who we *think* we should be and spot every fault and failure. No one wants to feel judged like that, and so we don't like looking too deeply at ourselves. But it's vital to figure this out early. It's the foundation that a good life is built on.

   Task: *In the appendix of this guide is a chart of values. Find a private place where you won't be interrupted while you mull over which ones best fit you. This is a deeply personal process and no one else needs to know what you come up with if you don't want to share.*

   On your first pass through the list you'll probably end up with a lot of values that are derivatives of each other, but one will stand out as the truest fit. To really hone in on what's most important, you'll want to narrow it down to no more than seven or eight. Remember that you're looking for the ones that really click, not just ones that your family would be proud of or that would make you look the best to your coworkers.

   Set the list aside and come back to it a few times over the course of a week to ensure your mood on one particular day doesn't make the decisions for you. It's possible that as you do the rest of the work in this book you'll end up refining your values as you learn more about yourself, but unlike goals and dreams they won't change on a regular basis. If it seems like they do, then you haven't gotten to the core and have some reflecting to do.

   When you're finished, think about ways you can bring your life closer in alignment with your values. When we live according to our values, we naturally feel satisfied at the end of the day even if our circumstances aren't ideal.

   The person who values Love highly but doesn't have a partner right now will be happier if they strengthen the platonic relationships in their life in the meantime—not all love is romantic. Someone who values Diversity might feel trapped in a job that never varies from day to day, but while they look for a better fit they can change up the routine at home to increase their sense of well-being. One of my values is Adventure, and while I was saving up the funds to travel full-time I took weekend trips to fulfill that desire.

Step 2: Remember how to dream

A lot of dissatisfaction arises from the gap between what a person holds dear (their values) and what they spend the majority of their time doing (their circumstances). It's time to change that. This is a fun step we're going to discover what you want from your life, your dreams for the future. The goal here is to bring our personal and professional lives more in line with who we are. For many people, this means dropping 'earning more money' as the priority in life, unless one of your values happens to be money-oriented.

As children, we have a lot of dreams. As we grow up, we slowly lose sight of them as we learn that one must be practical to survive in the real world. Following your heart and doing what you love is seen as a nice idea in theory but not something that's attainable for the average person Except, there is no rule. The only person whose permission you need to change your life is your own.

Task: *It's time to take a page from childhood and remember how to dream. Take out a piece of paper or open your word processor and ask yourself what you've always wanted to do, what you want to be remembered for, and what gifts you have that you want to share with the world. Make a list of what comes to mind.*

Don't be afraid of putting too many things down. This is the start of what's commonly called a bucket list, or a dream list, and it should be full of goals and dreams-enough to last a lifetime. Maybe the places you've always wanted to visit, hobbies you've been wanting to take up, the foods you've always wanted to cook.

Forget about what you think is realistic and let your heart be your guide. For some people, just learning that it's okay to dream is enough to get them started on dreaming big, but for others it may take a little time. Maybe you want to change careers, create a community with far-reaching aims, or become fluent in another language. For now, don't worry about the *how*. That will come later.

If you find you're having trouble writing down anything other than simple dreams, try writing your list somewhere away from home, or just after finishing an activity that inspires you. Get your creativity flowing and unblock your sub-conscious where you've probably already given some thought to what you really want to do with your life but told yourself you couldn't or that it wouldn't be proper. The value of a dream should be based on how good it makes you feel, not how socially acceptable it is or whether it has an outward purpose. Think of *internal* value. And yes, do get in touch with your inner child! It's possible that some of the stuff you dreamed of back then are things you still want deep down. Nothing is too small, big, or crazy to make it onto this list.

While you're working on it, give some thought to dreams that help others as well as yourself. A lot of times, people don't think about giving back until after they've attained some measure of success. This is fine, but working contribution in at the start of the process grants the opportunity to integrate it directly with your dreams. Chances are you have some gift, skill, or knowledge that you hold dear, and finding a way to share it would not only make a difference in the life of someone else, but improve yours as well. Contribution feels *good*, especially when you do it from the kindness of your heart and expect nothing in return.

Unlike your guiding values, your dreams will and should change regularly. Your dream list will evolve over time as new interests arise to replace old and completed ones, but do check for a correlation between dreams and values. That's a good sign that they are more than a whim and something you truly want. If you find you have a lot of items on your dream list that aren't related to your values, stop and take stock. You might be tempted to put things on your list like those status symbols mentioned in the introduction, or goals that will make you look good to others, but the happiness gained won't be as lasting and meaningful.

Once you have a handle on your list, don't wait to get started. It's likely some of the simpler dreams are achievable right now. On the road to great things, small accomplishments in the beginning can have a bigger impact than the big ones we eventually get to, because the small stuff changes our outlook and gets us thinking about life in a different way.

Step 3: Figure the cost

People often contact me for advice through my blog, and the number one excuse I've heard that keeps people from their dreams is money concerns. It's a fear born of our cultural mindset of scarcity, that we never have enough. The best way to quiet that concern is to figure out how much each of your dreams is going to cost. Once there's a number assigned to a dream, it cuts through fear of the unknown and makes the dream easier to grasp.

Task: *Go through your bucket list and pinpoint the ones you want most, then start researching the price. It's best to do this for several dreams at once, we'll get to the reasons why in a bit.*

If the dream is something you want to own, shop around to get an idea of the price tag. If it's something more complex, like taking a trip, break it down into each facet. Research the cost of gas or plane tickets, the accommodations once you're there, and the food and entertainment you want to partake in. If the dream is less tangible or has too many facets to be able to accurately account for, find as many other people as you can who have achieved the goal and learn how much it cost each of them them to get a ballpark figure.

Don't rush through this process. The more effort you put into the research, the more likely you are to find better deals or extra perks, and pinpoint exactly what you want from the dream.

If there's a wide range of price points to choose from, consider this:

There's a story I read once that really stuck with me, about a young man at a business conference who approaches his role model after a presentation for some advice. He wants to be a millionaire so he can have the best life possible. His idol asks him what he will do once he has a million dollars. The young man is stopped short: clearly he hadn't given it much thought. "I'd go fishing," he says at last. "I love fishing." His idols smiles and says "Well, you don't need a million dollars to go fishing." A few years later, the business guru hears from the young man again. He'd changed tactics and was no longer spending all of his time trying to earn a million dollars. Instead, he had cut back his hours so he could do more fishing. He was a lot happier.

There's a lesson to be learned here. As a culture, we tend to want the best money can buy, at least within our price range, but that might not always be the best answer. Think back to your economics class in school, and the concept of opportunity costs. Money is a renewable resource—when you spend it you can always go make more.

But making money has an opportunity cost, which is your time.

Unlike money, time is a non-renewable resource, and its sneaks by faster than we realize. Only once time has started to run short do we realize how important it is. I'm sure you've heard stories about people on their death beds who wished they had done more with their lives and taken a few more chances. No one ever wishes they'd spent more time working. It all comes back to that story: if you spend all your time making money, you end up with less time to enjoy it.

In the end, it's up to you to decide how much time you're willing to trade for money. When you're researching the price range of the various dreams on your bucket list, ask yourself whether you want to pay top dollar for the best, or if spending less will still fulfill the dream to your satisfaction. I personally value time higher than money, so I live simply and the majority of my dreams have more modest price tags. Having plenty of free time to pursue my own interests is invaluable to me.

Once you've picked a price point to aim for, whatever it may be, write it down so that you have a clear goal. Put it right on your bucket list, so that it's easy to compare the costs of your dreams and decide in what order you'd like to fulfill them.

Even looking for less expensive ways to meet your dreams, some of them might be so pricy that they seem out of reach right now. I pegged my cost of going full-time RVing at $17,500 which is no small sum for a person who's made no more than $29,000 a year her whole adult life.

The topic of personal finance is a large one, and there are plenty of resources out there offering good information from books to classes to websites. Enlisting the aid of a professional also may be warranted, depending on your situation. As a disclaimer, I am not qualified to offer financial advice, but from my personal experience you'll want enough money for the following:

1. The cost of the dream
2. Your living expenses
3. Saving for the future
4. An emergency fund (if the dream has a degree of risk)

The first step is to figure out where you are now, financially.

If you don't already do so, start keeping track of your monthly expenses and income. You can use spreadsheets or purchase software that will help with this, but I kept it simple by having one checking account that has a debit card tied to it, that all of my money goes into and comes out of. At the start of every new month I go back over my bank statement and tally up everything I bought and how much I made, and that gives me my cost of living and income. Do this for several months because there will be fluctuations, and you'll get a good picture of how long it'll take you to meet the monetary goal of your dream if nothing changes.

If you don't like how long it's going to take to get the money you need, there are essentially two choices. The first thing to do is look at living expenses and make cuts where you can.

Look over your receipts to see what you spend your money on and ask yourself how much value you're really getting for the money, compared to how much value fulfilling your dream would give. It's easy to spend $4 on a latte—it doesn't seem like much—but if you do that three days a week before work, that's $12. Four weeks a month, and that's $48. How much better would you feel if you made your own coffee in the morning, knowing you'd achieve your dream that much faster?

I got in the habit of making myself wait at least a week before a purchase of over $15 and discovered that after a week I usually didn't want the item bad enough anymore to spend the money on it. Impulse buying all but ended.

Recurring expenses and subscription services are also something to look at. Review them and make sure you're not still spending money on something you've lost interest in. Check to make sure there aren't better options available for your phone and internet plan, as prices on those change regularly. Eating out less and planning grocery trips are another great way to cut back on costs.

The second option, of course, is to make more money. This is a little trickier because remember, to make more money you need to spend time. If you really enjoy your job and you would get additional fulfillment or personal value by working extra hours, more power to you. But in many cases, working extra hours at a day job decreases happiness significantly and adds to stress. It might be necessary in the short term to save the funds needed for a dream, but in the long run the negatives would likely outweigh the positives.

But working extra hours at a day job isn't the only way to bring in more money. Take an inventory of your belongings and see if there's anything you no longer need or want that can be sold.

Think about your guiding values and look at your dream list. Do a little brainstorming to see if there's a way you could earn some extra money doing something you enjoy. Do you love animals? Cars? Music? Crafts? Could you get a part-time job, or do some other work that incorporates one of your interests?

Even if it will take a while to start earning money from your interests or hobbies, consider starting on it now, because there's nothing as rewarding as getting paid to do what you love.

Step 4: Reclaim your time

The world is speeding up. We rush from place to place, and even with the modern convenience of microwaves, cars, laundry machines and computers, there is still never enough time. You now have a list of dreams you'd like to see accomplished and the knowledge of how much they'll cost, so the next step is finding the time to work on them.

There are three key points here: Time management, efficiency, and prioritizing.

We all know at least one person who always seems to get twice as much done as everyone else. Those hyper-productive people have learned how to prioritize what matters most to them and cut out everything that doesn't help achieve their goals. They combine and streamline tasks to make the most efficient use of their time, and they're very good at managing their time and scheduling so that time-wasters don't creep in.

Task (part 1): *To get started, write down the schedule of everything you do in a day–from showering to eating, commuting to work, reading your e-mail, everything–and note the time when you start and stop each activity. Do this for several days, because your routine will vary from day to day.*

At the end of a week it should be pretty clear where your time is going. Items on that schedule will generally fall into two categories: things you *need* to do, and things you *want* to do.

The Needs will be necessities like paying bills, grocery shopping, and working. The Wants are activities you do for the pleasure of it, like hobbies, going out to eat with friends, and reading a good book.

Task (part 2): *The best thing you can do to reclaim your time is prioritize what matters most and subtract fillers from your life. So take a look at your schedule and* *ask yourself: What am I doing now that doesn't add value to my life?*

Maybe you read a periodical that hasn't really captivated you for some time now, but you continue in the hopes it'll get better again. Maybe you turn on the TV even when there's nothing good on. Maybe you spend a lot of time on Facebook keeping up with the statuses of your 500 friends—most of whom you don't really know. Maybe you hang out with coworkers once a week out of obligation to the team, but you don't enjoy the experience.

Yes, it isn't only tasks you want to think about. This advice applies to people and relationships too, which is hard for some to grasp. If a person is taking up your valuable time and not giving you value in return, it's okay to spend less time on that relationship—barring dependents of course. You can still love someone without them being a staple in your life.

Often though, the biggest time-wasters are the internet and television that we go to when we don't feel like doing anything else. It may be easy to veg out in front of a screen, but now you know what you really want to do with that time. Be ruthless in saying "no" to activities and habits that no longer serve you. In the end, you'll have much richer memories for getting out and taking an active hand in your life rather than just being an observer.

Task (part 3): *Once you've cut out everything you can, the next step is to increase efficiency by reducing the time spent on chores and combining similar tasks together.*

It never occurs to most people to question the way they have always done things. Thinking outside the box isn't just a great way to approach life in the broader sense, it's also a great way to approach the more mundane tasks of living. Just because we've always done a chore a certain way doesn't mean that's the fastest way. Do some experimenting and see if you can't find a shortcut. Work smarter instead of harder. Not every experiment will be a success, but even failure imparts wisdom. As a single person, cooking every day wasted a lot of time on an activity I'm not fond of. So now I make meals with two or three servings, and this more than halves my cooking time for the week.

For tasks that require thought and focus, do the whole task in one sitting when possible. This eliminates the need to remember where you left off and getting back into the right frame of mind. Activities that require a lot of prep or cleanup also benefit from being completed in one session.

The internet has made a lot of mundane chores easier to fulfill. Instead of running to the bank to deposit a check or running to a store to check for a specific item, can you do your banking online, or look at the store's website to make sure they carry the item before you make the drive?

Think about chores that can be grouped together. If you need to drive into town to pick up bread and milk, do every task that needs to be done in town, even the ones that don't need to be be taken care of immediately. This saves on gas *and* time. Consider designating one day a week as a cleaning day, ideally on a laundry day. A lot of cleaning can be done between changing loads, making use of a block of time not large enough for more involved tasks—a block of time that might otherwise go to waste on time-fillers.

Instead of opening your e-mail and Facebook multiple times a day, just check it once a day and take care of all responses at that time instead of coming back to them later. It can also be beneficial when going online to give yourself a time limit or a list of what you intend to get accomplished to avoid getting distracted and surfing aimlessly.

Once you've cut out the time-fillers that don't serve

your new goals, grouped together your chores, and thought about more efficient ways of doing them, look at what's left on that schedule. The gaps that have opened up from the work in this section are where you'll find the time for your dreams. Hold onto that schedule, because we'll be building on it in the next step.

Step 5: Skip the stress, plan instead

Having freed up the time to work on them, many bucket list items come easily. But there's still one category of dream we need to talk about: the big, life-changing ones that can take a year or more to make a reality. I'm going to refer to these big dreams as *life goals*. Chances are you have at least one of them on your bucket list. Examples include playing an instrument or sport at a professional level or starting a business.

During our school years we're given plenty of homework that can be completed in a day (marathon crunch the night before it was due, anyone?), but when faced with big projects like life goals that truly take months or years to complete, we're not very well prepared. Some have learned these skills by necessity, but a lot of people have never had the opportunity.

These kind of dreams require more than just time: they demand some structure too. Life goals by their nature are going to have multiple facets, and likely a lot of steps to see them to completion. This is where planning comes in.

Let's start by taking your big goal and breaking it down into a list of chronological steps. We're going to call this your Life Goal Checklist and it's a separate entity from the schedule started in Step 4.

__Task (part 1):__ Think about your life goal and the steps you'll need to take to make it a reality. This can be frustrating because there's usually a lot of uncertainty around big dreams. You likely don't know exactly how you're going to achieve your life goal at this point, and that's okay. This will help with the confusion. Don't get into detail right now, that will come later. Just list the major steps. You can do this on a piece of paper or word processor.

If you're having trouble listing the steps in order chronologically, try working backward instead. Imagine having just completed your goal—what step did you just finish to get here? And keep going back from there.

Task (part 2): *Once you have a general idea of the order things need to happen in, simply make a checklist out of them. Leave plenty of space between each item so you can fill in more detail and add additional steps if necessary. You want it to be simple and uncluttered, so that it's clear what needs to get done next. This will make it easier to track your progress and prove to yourself that you are making progress.*

The beauty of this checklist is that it keeps you from having to approach your life goal as one big, daunting project. The only thing you need to worry about is that very next step you need to take. If that next step is still too large or complex to act on, here is where you break it down until you get to a point where just a single action is required to move forward. When you know exactly what action you need to take next, it eliminates a lot of the stress. And when that step is complete, just look at the next one. As an example, I've included my RVing checklist from mid-January of the year I started full-timing in the appendix.

Sometimes while you work, ideas will come to you, things you need to do further down the line or something you want to research further. Don't lose your place to jump on these ideas, add them to your Life Goal Checklist where they fit chronologically. It doesn't pay to research steps further ahead than where you are in the process now, because you'll likely forget the nuances of what you've learned by the time you need to act on that information. Just focus on the step you're currently on.

Next we'll pull back and look at your day as a whole, so head back to that schedule you made in the last section of how you spend your day. You should now have a good idea what chores and other tasks need to get done on a certain day, how long those tasks will take, and how much free time you have to work on your bucket list.

Your schedule can be as simple or complex as you want to make it. There are whole books out there devoted to planning, even software you can buy and spreadsheets you can fill in. None of that worked well for me because it felt like I spent more time planning than actually doing. Everyone organizes differently though, so if the following advice doesn't fit your style, know that there are plenty of other systems out there just an internet search away.

Remember how we assigned schedule tasks as Needs or Wants? A lot of people who fail to achieve their life goals make the simple but devastating mistake of categorizing them as a Want, and then they wonder why they never seem to make any progress on it. To make regular progress on your life goal, you should prioritize it as a Need–as important as your job or doing laundry.

This means you won't have the free time that your friends have for relaxation and fun. You'll have to leave more Want items off your schedule for now, but trust me (and yourself) that this hard work will pay off with dividends later when you're living a life you love and your peers are still trapped just going through the motions.

I do best when I have a good chunk of time for working on life goals–at least an hour and a half– because it takes me a while to find my groove and get focused. So I try to pile as many weekly chores into one day as possible, to free up at least an hour and a half on other days to work on these checklist items. Some days I won't have time for any, but when I do work on it I'll do several in a row.

Other people find their focus quickly and put out their best work early in a session, so for them having smaller blocks of time more frequently during the week works best. That, or taking a larger chunk and breaking it up into smaller ones with breaks in between.

No matter how your attention span works, keeping focus is key. Edge past your productivity window without taking a substantial break to refuel your physical and psychological tanks, and you're just serving time. I like writing blog posts all in one sitting, but some of the longer ones might take up to four hours to complete and very few people (myself included) can stay focused that long. So I'll work a 15-minute break in to get up and stretch and do something else for a bit.

As to what should go where in your daily schedule, that's dependent on your own cycle. Many people experience a lull in energy and focus right after lunch, so why so many businesses schedule meetings for that time is beyond understanding. Some people are more productive right away in the morning and some can work well into the evening. You'll need to schedule some of your chores for certain times of the day when businesses are open, for instance, but the work that requires the most energy and concentration (life goal work), should happen during your most productive time of the day when possible.

Even prioritizing your life goal as a Need, sometimes several days may go by where you aren't able work on it and that's okay, as long as you don't use that as an excuse not to work on it at the next opportunity. We tend to overestimate what we can do in a day and underestimate what we can do in a year. Even if you can only spare three hours a week to work on a life goal, that adds up over time. The biggest journey starts with but a single step. Just focus on one life goal at a time and keep up that momentum. You'll be amazed at where you find yourself in a month, and eventually in a year.

Step 6: Take the plunge

Most often, the early to-do items on a person's Life Goal Checklist are information-gathering in nature, a discovery of how to go about undertaking this big change. Research is very important and shouldn't be overlooked, but there is such a thing as letting this period drag on beyond usefulness.

At some point, you're going to take one more small step as you've been doing all along, and find that you've made more progress than you've realized. There will come a time when that next step cannot be easily revoked and all of your effort is put to the test. Moments like these can be likened to taking a step off a cliff and hoping that the parachute you've fashioned will function properly.

For going full-time RVing, that step was when I was presented the paperwork to trade in my car for the truck that would tow my future trailer. For starting my blog, it was when I hovered over the "Publish" button on my first post. For writing my first book, it was the day I announced the release date to the world.

Reaching that juncture where you're about see a change in your daily life is very exciting, but also rather scary. A lot of people hit a wall here and stall out on their big dreams, saying the timing isn't right. They get caught in a loop of endless fact-finding and tell themselves they'll take that next step once they know everything will turn out according to plan.

The truth is, it's impossible to have all the answers about life goals at the start, and there will always be distractions.

The good news is that your research and plan don't have to be perfect. Instead of saying "I don't know," say "I'll figure it out." Destinations are reached by walking, not by endlessly plotting a course. It may be hard to commit to finishing right now, but **do** commit to starting. Real data obtained along the way will provide the feedback needed to fill in the knowledge gaps. Take the plunge and don't worry about trying for perfection. Start anywhere, and adjust course as you go.

Task: *Choose imperfect action. Remember that time is the most precious resource we have, so the sooner you get started the better off you'll be.*

Part 2
Problems You'll Face
(and how to overcome them)

Once you move from the discovery phase into the action phase of your big dream, the stakes become higher. You'll continue to schedule and use your checklist to ensure progress, but problems are going to start cropping up that cannot be prepared for ahead of time.

It's a lot like a roller coaster ride. There will be breathtaking highs where it feels like anything is possible, and earth-shattering lows where you doubt everything you're doing. This part of achieving your dreams can be exhilarating and terrifying at the same time, but with the proper tools and support, the hurdles aren't as tough.

Part 2 is all about solutions for the most common problems that arise when tackling life goals and other big dreams. We'll talk about fear, risk, exposure, overwhelm, finding support, and how to pivot if it looks like a dream isn't viable.

The obstacle of yourself

One of the largest stumbling blocks on the road to our big dreams is ourselves. That old adage "you are your own worst enemy" has more than a shred of truth to it.

We audit our thoughts constantly, judging our ideas and desires as right or wrong, practical or impractical, often without being completely conscious of it. Internal self-criticism keeps us from doing silly or stupid things like telling the boss what we really think about having to work an extra shift, or leaving the house in a t-shirt when it's below freezing outside. It has its uses, but can be damaging to big dreams.

This decision process is made based on three things: past experiences, cultural wisdom, and knowledge we have gained. So when a person contemplates a life goal that goes against cultural wisdom, that they have no experience with, and do not have all the answers for, that little part of the brain that judges practical from impractical is going to say no, it can't be done. And that doubt will keep coming back, fading into the background when things are going well but leaping forward when the going gets tough.

We need to listen to our thoughts objectively instead of taking the "I can'ts" to heart, and know that these doubts are not set in stone.

If the decision to put on a jacket when stepping into the cold had to be reasoned through on every occurrence, that would waste a lot of time. So our clever brains create shortcuts, choosing the way to react based on past stimulus so that it becomes a habit. All a habit is, is a repeated thought. When you become aware of this process, you can change the habit by not choosing the shortcut and by responding differently. Act on the thoughts that go along with what you want instead, and ignore or transform the rest. Do this for long enough, and a new shortcut develops that helps instead of hinders.

Even obstacles that seem like they're beyond our control are within our ability to shape. It just requires looking at the situation a different way. Life is 10% what happens to us, and 90% how we react to it.

While we cannot control everything in our lives, we certainly are in charge of how we respond. Two men miss a connecting flight home to their families because of delays. One gets angry and has heated words with the teller behind the counter because the next flight out is hours away, while the other accepts the news with stoicism. Did the person who reacted negatively feel any better for yelling? Not likely, and he probably experienced more pain that the person who took it in stride and accepted that the situation was one he couldn't change and so there was no point in getting upset.

If you believe the world is out to get you, it will color everything that happens to you. Setbacks will be proof that your dream isn't possible, and you'll have trouble seeing the opportunities life presents because of the negativity you're carrying.

Ultimately though, you are responsible for you. Blaming society, your family, or the government (things outside your circle of influence) for your situation gets you nowhere. Successful people realize that *they* decide on the contents of their life. Instead of complaining about lack of resources, they're resourceful. They don't lament the bad hand they've been dealt: they celebrate getting to play it how they like.

You are not just a product of your environment–your environment is also a product of you. When you stop using others as an excuse for why you can't, it's amazing how much easier progress comes.

In the end, there's only two critical things you need to make your dreams a reality, and if you listen to nothing else in this guide I hope you'll listen to this: **You need a dream, and you need persistence.** That's it. If you're dedicated to seeing a project through, all other problems can be overcome.

Managing fear and risk

Big dreams aren't safe. Nearly all of them have some degree of risk involved, and many don't follow a template with the steps clearly laid out. In the unknown lies limitless possibility, but also a lot of anxiety and resistance. About the same time we realize how far out of our depth we are, fear steps in to undermine our ability to move forward.

It's a problem with multiple causes, the first of which is our natural aversion to what we don't know. Life goals often require a person to spend an extended amount of time in limbo with a great amount of uncertainty. It can be very challenging to go from the stable environment of the status quo to the highly unstable environment of big dreams, but you can increase your tolerance to uncertainty by getting used to taking small risks first.

- Try a different brand of something you buy regularly
- Talk to strangers in line at the grocery store
- Visit that restaurant you always drive by but have never stopped at before
- Contact that friend you lost touch with years ago

The second problem is fear. Everyone experiences fear at some point in their lives, even the rich, famous, and fulfilled. There's no way to get rid of it completely, but in many situations fear can be helpful.

Since fear often accompanies the unknown, it pushes us to think critically about a situation (like life goals) where we don't know all the answers, and it can be a great motivator to overcome inertia and adapt to problems.

A writer who fears their book being laughed at will work more diligently on it. Parents worried about moving will be more thorough searching out a good neighborhood for their kids. An employee who's uncertain about his or her performance at a new job will try harder to learn the ropes. You'll notice all of these examples can be boiled down to the same thing: fear of failure.

Absolutely, you are going to make mistakes pursuing your life goal. Everybody makes mistakes sometimes, and that's okay because that's how we learn. There's a big taboo against failure in our country that hurts us more than it helps, because it makes us afraid to even try. Missteps are often not as final and devastating as they're made out to be, and the only way you truly fail is if you stop trying.

Just as we're in charge of how we react to situations beyond our control, we're in charge of how we react to failure as well. In fact, we're free to define failure however we want. Treat it as a learning experience and it loses much of its sting. Never be afraid to fail better. Yes, it's true that others get to decide for themselves how they define failure too, and part of the stigma of failure is wondering what others will think of us, but we'll get to how to handle those people soon.

In the meantime, let's turn that fear surrounding your life goal into a tool and put it to good use.

Task (part 1): *Make a list of everything you worry about going wrong with your life goal, big or small. Do you have plans in place should these things come to pass?*

If not, work down your list and come up with a solution for each.

Some potential problems are easy to mitigate, but the greater the degree of risk involved, the more involved the plan will have to be. When I was preparing to go RVing, I worried about the 13-year-old RV I was interested in buying having a problem that would be expensive to fix. To avoid a lemon, I downloaded a checklist of things to look at in a used RV and asked a lot of questions of the owner, but I still worried about the purchase, even after my thorough investigation turned up no issues.

This RV would become my home and a lot was riding on it functioning well, so because of the high degree of risk involved I put aside $5,000 in savings. This I dubbed my emergency fund, not to be touched unless some unexpected problem came up. Even having taken these measures, the fear of something breaking never completely went away (it still hasn't!), but it inspires me to stay on top of routine maintenance no longer keeps me awake at night because I know I'll be able to take care of it should something happen.

The trick to keeping fear from blowing out of control is to do **everything you reasonably can** to assure that your venture will turn out the way you want it to. If you've done your research and put in the best effort you can, given the circumstances, then there's no point in worrying further.

Sometimes though, fear still creeps in when we have a slow moment, or when lying in bed at night. Often these worries are irrational, causing concern about things that can't be prepared for. This type of fear is not productive. It's the kind that feeds on itself, without giving feedback you can use to overcome it.

When it comes to life goals, irrational fear tends to culminate in the Worst-Case Scenario. Our brains are experts at thinking up the absolute worst thing that could happen to us, and waving it in our faces as a reason why we shouldn't try X, Y, or Z. Call it the safety defense, an old survival habit from back when our ancestors were still swinging in trees and primal fear kept us safe from predators. If you don't know the outcome of what you're thinking of doing, best to stick to what's safe and not try it at all.

But we're capable of reasoning and thinking ahead, and the dangers of the modern world are less harsh than they were while we were evolving. The Worst-Case Scenario for your big dream is highly unlikely to leave you dead, which is what this defensive mechanism is trying to protect you against.

Trying to reason with irrational fear when you're in its grip is all but impossible though, so it's time for another exercise. This one has three parts.

Task (part 2): *First, write out the worst case scenario for your big dream. The absolute worst thing* *that could go wrong with it, the deepest fear that keeps you awake at night.*

For RVing, mine went something like this: Unable to find work, I run out of money and my truck breaks down somewhere remote. I don't know anyone in the area, and when I call my friends and family up on the phone to ask for help they just laugh and say it's my own fault. I have to pull what I can carry out of the RV and I end up living under a bridge, starving and destitute.

Having already come up with solutions for potential problems with your life goal as discussed above, it's unlikely you'd ever get in such dire straits. To prove it to yourself, make notes of all the measures you've taken to ensure your worst-case scenario never comes to pass.

Let's go back to my RVing example.

1. I decided I wouldn't travel to a new area if I didn't already have a job lined up there, so I wouldn't even be on the road if I was in danger of running out of money.
2. My emergency fund was large enough to cover almost four months of living expenses, so even if it took me a while to find work, I wouldn't starve.
3. If I found myself without a job, I was dedicated to treating job searching like a full-time job itself, spending 40 hours a week on applications and not being picky about what kind of work I took.
4. If all else failed, my parents and friends would bail me out if I needed them to. I might get a talking to about being irresponsible and it would be uncomfortable, but remember, we're talking about the absolute worst here.

When you lay out the reasons why your worst-case scenario won't happen in a matter-of-fact list, it does a lot to halt the cycle of worry and diffuse irrational fear.

There's also a trend that is easy to spot among worst-case scenarios: They all involve cases of bad luck compounding on each other. The probability of all of these problems happening at the same time is so small as to be insignificant. They also presume that when each problem surfaces, nothing is done to correct course before getting slammed by the next thing, which wouldn't happen in reality.

In fact, the very first part of my RVing worst-case scenario came to pass in my first six months on the road. I didn't yet know how hard it was going to be to find paying work for only half of the winter season. I waited too long to start looking, and found myself jobless at the end of my fall gig. Did I end up hungry and destitute under a bridge? Of course not, because I got serious about job-searching and didn't travel until I landed one.

Task (part 3): *The next thing to write out, is what would happen if you decided to stop following your dream.*

Remember the dissatisfaction you felt before this undertaking and think about what it would be like going back to the dull routine, back to wishing for something more. Likely your life goal is so much the epitome of your desires and values that, knowing now about a better way to live, it would be unthinkable to go back to what was. Imagine yourself years from now near the end of your life, and what your older self would think about this missed opportunity. Reminders of how dissatisfying life would be without big dreams makes it easier to push through fear.

Task (part 4): *And the last question: what would happen if your idea worked out?*

Instead of falling into the trap of dwelling on everything that might go wrong if you follow your dream (and remember, the chances of the absolute worst happening are very slim indeed), instead concentrate on what it would feel and be like if **it worked out**. If you are doing as much as you reasonably can to ensure success, this will be the more likely outcome. Give yourself permission to be excited, to think about the positives of your great idea, to daydream about it if that will help you to follow through.

Diffusing overwhelm

Related to fear and uncertainty, overwhelm is another obstacle commonly faced by those working on big dreams. While fear often stems from the unknown, overwhelm often stems from a lack of prioritization. If you've eliminated the time-wasters in your life and are scheduling your days like we talked about in Part 1, half of your battle here is already won. If it is a lack of time or structure causing the problem, then go back and review Steps 4 and 5 again.

People who are working on life goals are particularly susceptible to overwhelm. Not only are we engaged in the daily struggle of just getting by that causes so much stress, but the effort we put into big dreams and improving our situation places a lot of additional strain on us.

Let overwhelm take over, and it often manifests as a state where your brain is playing a loop of everything you need to get done, whether it's physical actions, research, or new problems that need to be looked into. Worrying about what needs to get done most keeps you from starting, and it becomes a cycle similar to the Worst-Case Scenario.

Stop what you're doing, and take five minutes to calm down (ten if you need it). And yes, I mean stop doing *everything,* including rehearsing in your head what you need to do when this little break is over. No matter how busy your day is, you do have ten minutes to spare to sort this out.

I usually focus on being present right where I am at that moment by paying attention to what I can see, hear, and smell around me (more about being present is coming up in Part 3), but if that doesn't work for you, think about something pleasant that is completely unrelated to your to-do list.

Once you're feeling more relaxed, pull out your schedule. Let's see about prioritizing the work that needs to be done to ensure the best use of your time.

All tasks have two basic values, whether you consciously assign them or not. One is how important the task is, the more important a task is—the sooner you should get it done (Needs vs. Wants). The other value is when that task is due. The sooner the due date, the sooner you should get it done—unless it has a low enough importance that it can be safely ignored.

Yes, sometimes the best way to solve the problem of overwhelm is learning to let go. A lot of times we assign a due date to something when there doesn't need to be one and create more work for ourselves. As you fill out your to-do list, you'll want to ask yourself if the task is something that really needs to get done.

For instance, when I was starting my blog I had a problem getting design and colors and fonts the exact way I wanted them, but I also had a lot of content to write and plugins and widgets to download and setting up the Facebook page and mailing list and numerous other tasks. Launching the blog on top of my full-time job was stressful and I was definitely suffering from overwhelm. I'd taken a week of vacation to do the launch, my to-do list was a mile long, and everything had to be done by that last day of vacation when I hit the 'publish' button on my first six posts and the blog went live.

Except that it didn't. I really wanted to make the blog look as professional as possible to make a good first impression on those early visitors, but that wasn't as important as having those first six blog posts be high quality. So I gave up on the problem of finding the perfect site design and it turns out it really wasn't a problem after all.

Tasks:

- *Make a list of everything that is making you feel overwhelmed, everything that you feel needs attention today, and prioritize it from most to least important.*
- *Add the most important things from your list into your schedule to be done first if they aren't there already. Forget about everything that isn't on your schedule to free up that mental bandwidth for what you need to get done now.*
- *As a test, try making a weekly schedule in addition to a daily one. It can help with overwhelm to be able to see what's coming several days down the road and knowing problems you can't get to today will be taken care of in due time.*

If you're still struggling with overwhelm frequently after these tips, it could be a sign that your work/life balance is off kilter. No matter how efficient a person is, there are limitations to the amount of work that can be accomplished in a day. Everyone has limits and it's not a sign of weakness to recognize this.

Improving the work/life balance

Some people need to stay busy to feel satisfied, but there is such a thing as taking it too far. It's not unusual for dedicated people to work through their vacation time and take very little sick or personal time. In our culture, working hard is seen as a moral obligation. If you're not always feeling at least slightly rushed, you're a slacker who is letting your family, your neighbors, and society down.

Plus, you know that working on your dreams is important, and as it is you feel like you aren't making quick enough progress. If you can load up your schedule with as much life goal work as possible, isn't that the fastest way to get to where you want to be?

The general consensus among high achievers is that true balance between work and play is all but impossible on a day-to-day basis, but it absolutely should be on a month-to-month basis.

Most life goals, flirting with the unknown as they do, require a lot more creativity and attentiveness than the average chore. To create something great, one cannot spend all their time working. Not only does it cause overwhelm and a diminishing of health and relationships, but it leads to an inferior end result. Great things require insight in addition to hard work, and insight doesn't come from checking things off a to-do list. Insight comes from living.

That part of the day you identified in Part 1 as being your least productive is the perfect time for self-care and recharging. Eat well, get enough sleep, and exercise. Get out and work on some of your simpler bucket list items, or things you enjoy that have nothing to do with your dreams at all. Gain some experience in the world's arena.

Staying motivated

Motivation comes easily at the beginning of a project when everything is new and exciting, but once the spark of novelty fades, it becomes harder to summon.

Some people might dismiss the idea of scheduling inspiration into the work day as new age mind-over-matter nonsense, but a person who is inspired will work harder and longer on their dreams. When you feel inspired, you don't have to force yourself to work on your life goal. It comes naturally as a result of your passion. Inspiration and motivation go hand in hand, and while motivation can originate from other sources (fear, pressure), coming to it through inspiration is the most pleasant.

First think of intrinsic motivation. Instead of working on a life goal simply because the schedule says it's time to do so, keep your guiding values in mind. Find the parallels between the actions you're taking to get to your goal and how those actions align with your values. For me, writing becomes less of a chore when I let my need for creativity and connection guide me. Worry less about the result, and find enjoyment in the steps you're taking now.

Also think of extrinsic motivation. Make time for the things that inspire you, especially when doubt, fear, or overwhelm threaten. We aren't machines that can continuously produce output without receiving input, and there is nothing weak about needing to refill our mental and emotional cups. A person can't give what they don't have.

- Listen to your favorite album
- Watch an inspiring video on YouTube
- Review a list of motivational quotes
- Create a collage of photos that remind you of your dreams
- Read a book (or blog) about someone who succeeded at the same goal you're pursuing
- Have a conversation with someone who's also pursuing their dreams

For the best result, set aside time for inspiration just before you work on your challenging dream or life goal, so that you start it with a firm resolve. Schedule it right along with life goal work, and treat it as seriously as you do work on your life goals.

Reactions to your dreams

The interpersonal side of life goals can be as big a worry as the dream itself, with questions like:

- When should I tell my family?
- What if people disprove of my dream?
- How do I find others who'll understand what I'm doing?

Generally, my recommendation is to have at least some of the research and planning done before sharing the news. Tell the important people in your life sooner rather than later if you believe they will react positively, or if what you're going to do will have a big impact on their lives. Wait if you believe they will act negatively as their doubt could make you doubt yourself which is no way to start a big project.

Now this is something of a simplification, because there is a whole spectrum of responses you could get from people when you tell them you're up to something unconventional.

Often, others won't fully understand the deep need to make this big change, but they'll still wish you the best with varying degrees of enthusiasm. Take note of the ones who seem genuinely interested in what you're up to and keep in regular contact with them—they can be a source of encouragement when you're hitting the rough patches.

Other people may react with indifference, which can be frustrating if it's someone close to you. We'll get to how to find people who will support you and understand what you're going through later.

Then there are those who react negatively. Now, a lot of times, close family members react negatively to big news of this sort because they're worried on your behalf, afraid of what will happen if your life goal doesn't work out.

This is why it's good to wait until you have a plan in place before sharing. Remember that fear is usually a reaction to the unknown, so a lot of times worry or slight disapproval can be turned into a more positive response by explaining the how and the why of the dream, and answering the questions that are troubling your friend or family member. Take the time to show them that this isn't just a whim and that you've put a lot of thought into it.

If that doesn't help, always remember that someone's response to your dreams, life, and beliefs is *their* problem, and not yours. On the opposite side of the coin, *your* reactions to others is *your* problem, not theirs.

Find common ground elsewhere and avoid the topic of your life goal unless you both enjoy debating. Just because they disagree, doesn't necessarily mean you need to cut them out of your life, although it might be good to limit contact with them until you're further along with your dream if their presence is going to make things harder for you.

And finally, there's the naysayers, the people who act downright hostile or with extreme skepticism when you tell them your plan. These kind of responses can be painful and bewildering, particularly if the person is someone you interact with regularly.

The best thing to do when faced with a naysayer is to ignore them and walk away. It might be hard, but their mind is already made up and trying to explain gets you nowhere with this group of people. All arguing with them will do is waste your time and energy and leave you frustrated.

While you can't change their opinion, it can be good for your peace of mind to understand why some people behave this way. It's impossible to know exactly what's going on in another person's head, of course, but here are two accepted theories.

The first is that these people don't believe they could improve their lives like you're working so hard to do, so to save their own fragile ego they push their inability onto others. It's a defense mechanism for those who are unhappy with their situation but not willing to change it.

People are very good at rationalizing their thoughts to cast themselves in a better light. We all want to be the hero in our own story, so someone who doesn't believe they can achieve something great will tell themselves (and you) that you can't either so that they can maintain that illusion.

The other reason is that some naysayers believe life to be a zero-sum game, that only a limited number of people in the world can be successful, so to increase their own chances at succeeding, they hope others around them will fail. These people are telling you you'll fail in the hopes you'll give up, and leave more slices of the proverbial pie on the table for them to reach for.

In some instances—like a traditional workplace for example—they'd be correct. There are only so many prime positions available at any given corporation, and a person might have to be not only ambitious, but willing to step on a few toes to secure one. But when you leave the arena of rigidly controlled environments like an office, there is no fixed number of slots for winners and losers.

Finding your tribe

Following your dreams can be a very lonely proposition if no one else in your life is as excited about this big change as you are. But there are others out there who share the same view, and seeking them out for moral support and guidance can be very beneficial.

The easiest place to start looking is online. Do a search for Your Thing, and see if you can locate websites, forums, Facebook groups or other communities about it. These kind of places are good sounding boards for any problems you might be facing, questions you want to ask of those further along in the process, and for a sympathetic listener when you need to share what you're going through.

Don't be afraid to reach out to a guru who's already been successful at your life goal or other big dream. E-mail is usually the easiest way—just be courteous and accept that it may take a while for them to get back to you, as they often have full lives. The worst that could happen is you don't get a response, which isn't the end of the world, and if you *do* get a response, it'll likely contain a lot of good information.

Depending on where you live, you might also be able to find local interest groups to join. You can check networking sites like Meetup.com and keep an eye out for conventions or events that people interested in your thing might be drawn to. Listening to the radio and looking at fliers is a good way to discover those.

If you prefer in-person connections to online ones but can't find anyone in your area with the same goals, all is not lost. Be honest about your dreams when having conversations with strangers. While hiding behind vague explanations and non-committal answers avoids confrontation with those who might not get you, it really stifles the soul after a while. It's incredibly liberating to be truthful to yourself, and putting your true self out there is an organic way to gently steer away those with whom you don't share much in common, and attract those who share similar views. Surround yourself with people who are taking a deliberate hand in their own lives and they'll likely be more supportive, even if their plans are different.

A word of caution though: Once you discover that life can be so much more than merely surviving, you may be tempted to shout your new philosophy to the world. But what lights you up won't light everyone up, so it's not a great idea to try to "convert" everyone you meet to your new way of thinking. You'll get more negative than positive responses. Everyone has their own path to walk.

When to quit, and when to press on

When the pressure of a life goal becomes too much, the

temptation to throw in the towel and go back to what's comfortable and easy becomes great—but that isn't always the right decision.

The desire to quit may come from an inability to handle the uncertainty, exposure, and risk of moving forward. It's also possible that the feeling is coming from the collection of enough data and experience to realize that the dream is unachievable as it stands.

Both are difficult problems, but not necessarily the end of the line.

We've already discussed techniques for increasing tolerance to uncertainty, mitigating risk by coming up with contingency plans, and how to handle naysayers who ridicule your dreams, but it's likely these themes will repeat themselves over the course of a big project and it doesn't necessarily get easier with time.

As for realizing your life goal isn't viable as is, often the plan you start with isn't the one you end up accomplishing. The less certainty there is around a dream, the more likely it will have to evolve from its original conception. Among inventors and creative types, these changes in direction are called pivots.

Let's say there's a person whose life goal is to be a paid artist and they plan to sell wares online, maybe at a store like Etsy. They're passionate about making wire-wrapped jewelry, but realize, once they've been at it for a couple of months, that it doesn't sell well enough to cover the cost of the materials and the time they put into it.

This person could pivot and take the dream in a different direction. Maybe the wire-wrapping they love to do doesn't sell well, but experiments with another type of jewelry show a lot more financial promise.

The question you need to ask yourself when considering a pivot is this: if you were to edit the dream significantly to make it work, would you still want the end result? In this case, would the artist still get enough satisfaction from serving their customers well, but in a way they're not as excited about? Don't simply show up and work on a dream without ever stopping to examine whether your current direction is still appealing to you.

When considering quitting altogether, the questions you need to ask yourself are very similar: is your heart still in it, or can you achieve greater results by moving on to something else?

Imagine yourself having just completed the life goal in question, post-pivot if that's the sticking point. All of the hard work has paid off, and you're enjoying the fruits of your labor. If you just see it in your head, that's a pretty good sign that you're no longer invested in the dream and it's time to move on. You'll find there's probably something else on your bucket list that is calling to you stronger.

But if you still feel it in your heart, that means you still want it. If your motivation for the dream is still intact at an equal or greater level than it was when you started, that's a good sign to keep pushing forward. If you quit now, it's possible there will be regrets later.

Trusting the process

Living deliberately is great for improving confidence, self-sufficiency and quality of life, but it doesn't change the core of who a person is. Any acquired baggage will still be there, and personality and general outlook on life will remain the same unless time is taken to learn new habits. These aren't things that can be "fixed" by external stimulus.

It can be frustrating, when you're taking baby steps toward your dreams and making mistakes to see other people who have succeeded or are further along than you are. It's a reminder of how much work you still need to get done, and can make you doubt yourself. You might envy their superior abilities or think they have some fundamental quality that you're lacking.

No one has a perfect life. Even those who make success look effortless have their own hardships and insecurities, it's just that those doubts and worries are kept internally, same as ours are. We only get to see a fraction of a person we don't know well, the best part that they choose to show the world, and it's all too easy to compare that best 10% of others to our worst 10% that we keep hidden.

What you don't know is that behind every success story was a lot of hard work and trial and error, just like what you're going through. There is no such thing as overnight success. The people who appear to have achieved it have done something similar before that gave them the skills and experience needed to have made quick progress this time around. The story of how they gained that understanding never makes nightly news—just the fantastic final product.

Working on life goals is bound to bring up some issues. You are not broken or wrong for deciding to quit a dream, for not knowing what exactly you want, or for not being completely satisfied upon completing a dream. We're constantly reinventing ourselves: the act of living is best viewed as road without end, and self-discovery works in the same way.

Never compare your progress, success, or situation to another's—compare it to where *you were* instead. Have faith in the process, and in yourself. We're stronger, wiser, and braver than we give ourselves credit for. Have patience, focus on what's in front of you, and stay strong.

One of the greatest lessons a person can learn is to be comfortable with themselves, and on the way to a better life, you'll hopefully glean a little insight into who you are.

Part 3
What Comes After

Congratulations, you've done it! You've seen several of your dreams come to fruition and life will never be the same. Is this Happily Ever After? There are two sides to every coin.

Don't settle

Implementing big changes in your life means an upheaval of everything you know. It's a time of excitement and wonder, but also of stress and risk. While the discomfort of the unknown is nearly always worth it in the end, it's hard to stay in the uncertainty zone for long stretches. Now that you've emerged on the other side, you're likely taking a break and congratulating yourself on a job well done.

That's a good thing, and you deserve some time to recoup and catch up on other areas of your life that may have fallen by the wayside while you've been working on a life goal—some of those Wants that you've had to put on the back burner for instance.

It may be tempting to coast and get comfortable. That's what most of the world does: settle for acceptable once they have what they can live with. At this point you've accomplished more than most people have, and you're ahead of the game. It would be all too easy to leave things where they are now.

But your dream list is still far from finished. In a couple of months once you've settled into a routine again that little voice will be whispering, *what next?* Novelty keeps our outlook fresh and there are always new challenges to

44

meet.

It'll be easiest to get started on new dreams sooner rather than later, while you still have momentum on your side. As we're always changing and growing, our dreams keep evolving right along with us. After completing a life goal or two, many feel called to build something around their dreams that will have a lasting impact, a legacy that may not change the world, but changes the world for those interested in Their Thing. In one sense, there is no happily ever after, because the next big dream is always right around the corner.

Life is a journey

On the flip side, for people who are driven by a need for constant improvement, it's easy to get caught up in an endless cycle of goals and achievements. When a life goal is completed, often the expected rush of accomplishment isn't as all-encompassing as we thought it would be. It doesn't satisfy the way we expected it would, given all that we put into it.

It's easy to believe that once you're living in alignment with your values and start achieving your big dreams relating to life, work, and play, you will love what you do 100% of the time. If you don't, it's seen as a sign you're not done yet and need to keep trying.

In the real world, that's not how it works. A dream job is one you like most of the time, love some of the time, and dislike on rare occasions. Just as there isn't a perfect time to get started on your dreams, you'll never have the perfect career, the perfect relationship, or the perfect life. It's good to seek improvement, but it's also possible to get so caught up in trying to make tomorrow the best it can be that you never enjoy today.

The real point of following our dreams is not to create a better future, but to cultivate a better present. Feelings of accomplishment and self-realization are just as much a by-product of the steps you're taking every day to achieve your dreams as they are a reward at the finish.

You know that old adage about stopping to smell the roses? It's a proverb about enjoying the moment, and there is a lot of wisdom to that advice.

We get so wrapped up in our story that we forget to look at the world at large. At first, we're too busy worrying about our bank accounts, what our neighbors think of us, and that the car is overdue for an oil change. After we start living deliberately, we worry about how to work on our dreams around other obligations, whether the dream will bring satisfaction, and whether the work we're doing will make a difference to others.

It's better to have the second set of problems than the first, but the result is the same: we live in our heads, instead of in the world.

Being present is about taking an active interest in what is around us, and it's a great practice to adopt. Here are some tips:

- Turn your full attention on someone when you're talking to them
- Ask yourself the why and how of the ordinary
- Slow down and engage in the world with all of your senses

Take some time every day to be grateful for what you have—your family and friends, your health, your home. Most of us have a lot more than we realize: we rarely give a thought to flush toilets, having enough money for groceries, and freedom of speech. It might sound counter-intuitive, but losing the expectations for what you're entitled to and understanding that everything you have is a gift to be cherished goes a long way towards a happier existence.

It's the dozens of little moments that make every day amazing, the ordinary ones with no big story to tell. Most people are too busy to enjoy the beauty of the sunrise during their morning commute, or the kindness of a stranger offering a helping hand. They may notice it, but the other thoughts clamoring for attention keep them from fully appreciating it.

Overcome the social stigma placed on being still and doing nothing. Taking some time every day to be quiet and observe is not the same thing as being lazy. It's okay not to be rushing around every minute of every day.

When you stop worrying so much about the future and combine learning to enjoy the journey with being present, great things happen.

There's a synergy between the two. When you tune out those distracting worries and thoughts about what comes next, and focus on the here and now, work on life goals and other dreams flows better because your brain is fully engaged with what you're doing.

The more you live in the present, the more joy you'll find. The more joy you find, the more effort and passion you'll naturally put into your endeavors. The more passionate you are in your endeavors, the more successful they'll be. The more successful they are, the the more fulfilled you'll feel.

So in the end, happily ever after is a frame of mind more than a destination. May the road be a long one.

Never stop dreaming,
Becky

Appendix

A list of values

Ability, abundance, acceptance, accomplishment, achievement, acknowledgment, adaptability, adequacy, adroitness, adventure, affection, affluence, alertness, aliveness, ambition, amusement, anticipation, appreciation, approachability, artfulness, articulacy, assertiveness, assurance, attentiveness, attractiveness, audacity, availability, awareness, awe

Balance, beauty, being, belonging, benevolence, blissfulness, boldness, bravery, brilliance, briskness, buoyancy

Calmness, camaraderie, candor, capability, carefulness, certainty, challenge, charity, charm, chastity, cheerfulness, clarity, classiness, cleanliness, cleverness, closeness, cognizance, comfort, commitment, compassion, competence, complacency, completion, composure, concentration, confidence, conformity, congruency, connection, consciousness, consistency, contentment, continuity, contribution, control, conviction, conviviality, coolness, cooperation, cordiality, correctness, courage, courtesy, craftiness, creativity, credibility, cunning, curiosity

Daring, decisiveness, decorum, deepness, deference, delight, dependability, depth, desire, determination, devotion, devoutness, dexterity, dignity, diligence, diplomacy, directness, discernment, discretion, discipline, discovery, diversity, drive, duty

Eagerness, economy, ecstasy, education, effectiveness, efficiency, elation, elegance, empathy, encouragement, endurance, energy, enjoyment, enlightenment, entertainment, enthusiasm, exactness, excellence, excitement, exhilaration, expectancy, expediency, experience, expertise, exploration, expressiveness, extravagance, extroversion, exuberance, evolution

Facilitating, fairness, faith, fame, fascination, fashion, fearlessness, fidelity, fineness, finesse, firmness, fitness, flexibility, flow, fluency, fluidity, focus, fortitude, frankness, freedom, friendliness, frugality, fun

Gallantry, generosity, gentility, genuineness, giving, grace, gratefulness, gratitude, gregariousness, growth, guidance

Happiness, harmony, health, heart, helpfulness, heroism, holiness, honesty, honor, hopefulness, hospitality, humility, humor, hygiene

Imagination, impact, impartiality, impeccability, independence, industry, ingenuity, inquisitiveness, insight, inspiration, instinct, integrity, intelligence, intensity, intimacy, intrepidness, introversion, intuition, inventiveness

Joy, judiciousness, justice

Keenness, kindness, knowledge

Lavishness, leadership, learning, liberation, liberty, liveliness, logic, longevity, love, loyalty

Majesty, mastery, maturity, meekness, mellowness,

meticulousness, mindfulness, moderation, modesty, motivation, mysteriousness

Neatness, nerve

Obedience, open-mindedness, openness, optimism, opulence, order, organization, originality, outlandishness, outrageousness

Passion, peacefulness, perceptiveness, perfection, perseverance, persistence, persuasiveness, philanthropy, piety, playfulness, pleasantness, pleasure, poise, polish, popularity, potency, practicality, pragmatism, precision, preparedness, presence, privacy, proficiency, professionalism, prosperity, prudence, punctuality, purity

Quietness, quickness

Realism, readiness, reason, recognition, recreation, refinement, reflection, relaxation, reliability, resilience, resolution, resolve, resourcefulness, respect, restfulness, restraint, reverence, richness, rigor

Sacredness, sacrifice, sagacity, saintliness, sanguinity, satisfaction, security, self-control, selflessness, self-realization, self-reliance, sensitivity, sensuality, serenity, service, sexuality, sharing, shrewdness, significance, silence, silliness, simplicity, sincerity, skillfulness, smartness, sophistication, solidarity, solidity, solitude, soundness, speed, spirit, spirituality, spontaneity, stability, stillness, strength, structure, substantiation, success, sufficiency, support, supremacy, surprise, sympathy, synergy

Tactfulness, teamwork, temperance, thankfulness, thoroughness, thoughtfulness, thrift, tidiness, timeliness, traditionalism, tranquility, transcendence, trust, truth

Understanding, uniqueness, unity, usefulness, utility

Valor, variety, victory, vigor, virtue, vision, vitality, vivacity
Warmth, watchfulness, wealth, wholesomeness, willfulness, willingness, winning, wisdom, wittiness, wonder, worthiness

Zeal, zest

A sample Life Goal Checklist

Traveling full-time in an RV

1. Continue downsizing
   * List PS2 and accessories on Craigslist
     - Make sure it all works first
     - Determine a price
   * Drop off clothing at Goodwill
   * Buy an e-reader and get rid of paper books?
     - Research brands
2. Get old 401k moved to current bank IRA. Maybe move to Simple Bank if it's out of beta and looking good by then?
3. Look into location independent income options
4. Determine mail forwarding solution (My Dakota Address or Alternative Solutions). Set up new address at least one month before departing to get everything switched to it!
5. Switch all bills/paper mail to electronic where possible, scan important documents and keep copies somewhere safe?
6. Move with J to small/cheaper living in September to work on savings
7. Buy laptop, look into Millenicom for Internet card

8. Decide on Insurance for RV/truck. Make sure it is full-timing insurance!
9. Decide on personal insurance–likely a high deductible plan through some company like BCBS
10. Buy Casita once circumstances allow (at least $16.5k if staying in one place for a while with steady income, 19k for traveling). See Purchasing Out of state document for details
11. Learn to drive the RV–attend a driving course or rally through Escapees?
12. Sign up for Escapees RV club and Passport America
13. Spend at least a couple months taking shakedown trips and determining what is needed for full-timing
14. Finish any necessary mods or repairs to RV
15. Plan first route before hitting the road (Escapees hypothetical trip planner?) including places to stop to earn income if needed (Quartzsite selling, working at Amazon, etc.)
16. Go to doctor and dentist before heading out
17. Quit job :)
18. Drive to SD to set up residency, get driver's license, vehicle and RV registration settled
19. Visit parents on first trip, drop off anything that needs to get stored & clean my room

Done:
- Decide on tow vehicle & RV
- Determine how much $ is needed
- Decide on state to "live" in
- Buy truck

About the Author

Becky Schade has been following her dreams since 2010 and has completed several life goals, including becoming a full-time RVer, being paid to sing at a renaissance festival, and starting a business around her passion of writing. She travels in a 17' camper trailer and enjoys being outdoors and sharing advice and adventures on her blog, www.interstellarorchard.com.

66266254R00030

Made in the USA
Columbia, SC
16 July 2019